Love Isn't Dying…

It Was Always Dead

Written by

Alexander Oliveros

Edited by

Ben Leach

ISBN: 979-8-9992891-0-0

Ebook ISBN: 979-8-9992891-1-7

Cover by Alexander Oliveros

Edited by Ben Leach

Published by Enter the Speedforce

2229 Peachtree Cir

Chula Vista, CA 91915

First Edition: July 2025

https://alexoliveros01.wixsite.com/alex-oliveros

To my parents,

Who have always loved and supported me.

Introduction

In the past couple of years, particularly in the post-COVID era, we've seen an increasing trend of young adults shifting away from seeking romantic relationships. This doesn't just mean your typical committed partners, this also means 'situationships' or even casual dating. In 2023, the Pew Research Center reported that roughly six in ten single people are not looking for a relationship or dates. To many people, this might sound quite alarming. Older generations worry future generations won't share vital parts of the human experience, arguably an important part of development. From those in younger generations still interested in romance, you'll often hear things like "Romance is Dying" or "Chivalry is Dead." "If things went back to how they used to be, things would be better, right?" While I certainly understand these concerns, I argue that love has never flourished like people claim.

Love isn't dying. No, it was always dead.

In this book, I'd like to explore the modern landscape of romance and how centuries of history have built up to our time (2025, if you're reading this in the far future). I'll be reviewing this through a Catholic lens and using straight relationships as my prime talking point, but I hope you can take something away from this book regardless of your background. This is also not a self-help book, at least in the traditional sense. I do not claim to know all the answers; every person is different and will have a different way of finding peace. I also write this book as a young man who has always been single. Some people might view that and think I shouldn't talk about this subject at all, but as Fink from the Wild Robot once said, "When you grow up without something you spend a lot of time thinking about it." I also want to preface this book by saying if you've engaged with any of the problems I will talk about, I do not blame you. This is a wider societal problem that affects each person differently, and the way each individual handles that will be very personal. I don't know your struggles or your life story, but I hope my talking points can be a consolation to you, especially if you feel hopeless in the pursuit of love.

With that, here are the main subjects I'll discuss:

If you've already made it this far, I want to thank you for picking up this book and reading it. It means a great deal to me! I've gone through so many struggles with romantic relationships. I felt called to write this book so I can hopefully help someone out there to navigate similar struggles. As I'll discuss later, there are a lot of predatory programs designed to prey off people desperate for love. Some are obvious scams, others are societal norms. Writing this was extremely therapeutic so no matter how many people read this, I want to thank you again for allowing me time to talk about love.

Chapter 1: The Jigsaw Flaw

Many years ago, I saw a comedy bit that I will never forget. This came from the Netflix Special "Jigsaw," hosted by Daniel Sloss. In it, Daniel describes a question he posed to his father when he was young: "What is Life?" His father would respond likening life to a jigsaw puzzle. Every person is creating their own jigsaw puzzle, each piece representing different experiences in life. The goal is to complete the puzzle of course, but the kicker is that no one knows what the picture looks like, so we just have to figure out where all the pieces go. The most sensible place to start is at the corners. These generally involve things like family, hobbies, your career. All these experiences start to shape who you are. Young Daniel then asked his father, "Well what's supposed to be at the center?" And his father replied, "that's your partner piece." According to this analogy, every one of us is destined to be with someone, our Soulmate. The puzzle will be complete once we find that person and happily spend the rest of our lives with them. Sounds great, right?

Daniel learned early on that this was an extremely harmful way of approaching life. The analogy implies that without our Partner Piece - without our Soulmate - we are imperfect. "We've been told that without someone else in your life, you're incomplete, you're broken. If you're alone, you are not whole." Now some of you might look at this and try saying Daniel's dad did a terrible job explaining life and romance. But unfortunately, this is a very common teaching. Our society tells us this exact thing all the time, even if it's not strictly about committed relationships. The only way we can be happy is if we have enough money. If we're in a relationship. If we have the right friends. If we have enough sex. If we have all the power in the world, that's when we'll be happy. As Daniel puts it, "We have romanticized the idea of romance, and it is cancerous."

This inherent flaw is central to everything else I will be discussing here. Needing something or someone else to make us happy is an inevitable dead end. We can lose our jobs. Friends leave. Our loved ones die. People change and we fall out of love. By having this mindset that we need a Partner Piece to be happy, we intrinsically believe we need more to be happy. More money. More Power. More Friends. More Muscles. More Intimacy. More. More. More. This is the path to the Dark Side. We become so consumed with what *we* need that we forget about the needs of others. It becomes our goal to take as much as possible, and this inevitably leads to physical and mental destruction. This book deals specifically with romantic situations, but almost every atrocity ever committed will lead back to this simple desire of finding "what makes us whole." Nearly everything on this planet is an insufficient way of finding that peace.

What I'm saying here sounds extremely nihilistic. For many years I lived with this jigsaw analogy in mind. For one reason or another, I have never been able to be in a romantic relationship. Maybe I was too awkward, maybe I wasn't forthgoing enough. Maybe someone did have feelings for me, and it flew over my head. Maybe it just wasn't the right time. I would constantly see other people in relationships. In real life, in movies, on social media. And I was always told that I *needed* to have a partner to be happy. A happy marriage was the end game, and the less time you spent pursuing that the higher your chances of dying sad and alone. I've tried changing myself "to get results." Different methods to try being in a relationship. Sadly, I admit I was almost led down a rabbit hole of incel culture that spewed horrible things about women. But whatever I tried, no matter how I changed my approach or my attitude, nothing seemed to work. After all this trying, I came to the conclusion that there was something inherently wrong with me.

You can all probably tell the danger of that conclusion. I'm lucky that I was never so hopeless that I wanted to hurt myself or others. But I fear others haven't been so lucky and meet a tragic end because of this. Unfortunately, there's been a number of shootings that have stemmed from this despair. Most notably, the 2009 and 2014 shootings committed by George Sodini and Eliot Rodger, respectively. Is there anything that can solve this? Do we just tell people to "tough it out" and move on? How many more tragedies need to happen before we can't brush it off any longer? Something has to change.

Daniel provides one answer. We must first love ourselves. "You need to learn to love yourself or you will employ someone else to do it for you." Loving yourself might sound selfish on the surface. However, this doesn't mean indulging in worldly pleasures. No, this means taking a look in the mirror, acknowledging your flaws, and accepting yourself for who you are. We are all broken people, there are things in the past and present we cannot change about ourselves. By learning to see ourselves and be happy in our situations, we learn to love others and the world. Of course, we should always strive to improve ourselves, but there is no such thing as a perfect person or a perfect life. If we cannot be comfortable being alone, then we are forcing someone else to fix some problem in our lives. Instead of working towards our own happiness, we make another person our anchor. We begin relying too much on that anchor, and we'll go through any lengths to make sure that anchor never leaves. This is a huge problem; one I struggled with for many years, and one I'm still trying to overcome. I was led to believe that by having a girlfriend or by having enough sexual encounters, *that's* when I'd stop being lonely. But I have realized continuing down that path would never make me fulfilled because I was seeking an insufficient form of love and validation. When I first looked at myself and truly saw all of me, that's when I began to heal myself. I don't need a girlfriend to be happy. I don't need to feel that embrace to be fulfilled. As long as I work on myself and do the best I can in the situations I'm given, I will be alright.

The Christian perspective asks us to take one step further. The Jigsaw Analogy is correct on some level: we are all imperfect and there is a void inside of us we continually seek to fill. Philosopher Blaise Pascal[1] gives a nice response to this.

> What else does this craving, and this helplessness, proclaim but that there was once in man a true happiness, of which all that now remains is the empty print and trace? This he tries in vain to fill with everything around him, seeking in things that are not there the help he cannot find in those that are, though none can help, since this infinite abyss can be filled only with an infinite and immutable object; in other words by God himself.

A more modern translation, one I like a bit better, says, "There is a God shaped vacuum in the heart of every man which cannot be filled by any created thing. But only by God, the Creator, made known through Jesus." So how exactly is this the case? Let's look to the Scriptures for help.

The Book of Genesis tells us the story of Adam and Eve. In the beginning, when God made the heavens and the earth, He created us in His image. The Garden of Eden was paradise, a place for God and Man to be in perfect unity with one another. There was no suffering, no pain, no loss. Only harmony with God. However, due to our arrogance and desire to become gods ourselves, we ate of the apple of the Forbidden Tree. We lost our innocence, knowing what's right and wrong, and we chose what's wrong for our own gain. This split us from God. He feared our fall would be permanent if we ate from the Tree of Everlasting Life. So, God banished us from the Garden of Paradise, pushed into the fallen world of our own creation.

---

1. Quoted from *Pascal's Pensées*, Section VII, 425.

Whether or not you believe this historically happened is not the point of the story. Humanity constantly chooses selfishness and darkness. Because of that separation from God, we are broken. This is why love was always dead. Due to our flaws, we are unable to love perfectly. We are always in conflict with our darker selves. The parts of us that want control, the parts that only care for the self. In every age, love has been twisted and distorted for the benefits of the powerful. Even for people with good intentions, we can't fully love properly because we've grown up in a world that's taught us to be selfish. From the moment Adam and Eve ate of the Forbidden Fruit, our capacity to love died.

But because God loves us, He had a plan to save us. The story of the Old Testament is God preparing the world for His rescue plan, which is eventually fulfilled in Jesus Christ. To complete the Jigsaw analogy, Christ is our Partner Piece. God is Love. Daniel's father was correct that love completes the Jigsaw Puzzle, but it could never be filled by any person or thing. Only God can do that. It is by understanding Him we learn to love again. It is through Him that we heal ourselves. He is our Redeemer. He makes us whole. Some of you reading this may be hesitant to follow Christ or even abjectly against the concept of following religion. What I'm trying to say here is that we need to overcome the self. We have to let go of our selfish desires and be a part of something greater than ourselves. Whether that be finding a purpose, connecting with nature, being one with The Force, reaching enlightenment. All these avenues point to a greater truth. I believe this means Christ is our Partner Piece. But regardless of your belief system, we do not need any earthly things to find our Partner Piece. Not any person, not any class, not even this book. You have the power to determine what that is. You have the power to find peace and happiness. You have the power to seek and understand truth. You have the power to change your life and the world for the better. That will give you much greater peace than any human relationship can.

So, as Daniel Sloss said, the first step to finding peace when it comes to romance is loving yourself. If we want to learn "how to love" or "how to be in love," we must first learn what love is. 1 Corinthians 13: 4-8 is a great quote that gives us some insight into this.

"Love is patient, love is kind. It is not jealous, it is not pompous, it is not inflated, it is not rude, it does not seek its own interests, it is not quick tempered, it does not brood over injury, it does not rejoice over wrongdoing but rejoices with the truth. It bears all things, believes all things, endures all things. Love never fails."

If our relationship with ourselves or with others contradicts this, then something is wrong. Because society pushes us to be in romantic relationships, we strive to be in one not because we want to but to appease others. Or worse, we're made to believe a partner is the only way to fulfill us, so getting that partner will appease us. This is inherently selfish. Because rather than picking a partner due to our undying love for them, we instead stay with them to make *us* happy. To appease *our* dreams and *our* desires or to make *our* image look better. Too many people pick the first person who accepts them and forces them to be their partner. Daniel Sloss explains that this phenomenon happens because we're so afraid of being alone that we'd rather have something than nothing. But again, no matter how well intentioned one might be in seeking a partner, this is inherently selfish. By trying to force someone to fit our Jigsaw Puzzle, we are creating inevitably terrible situations. Of course, this can end horribly with things like domestic abuse or cheating, but at its most basic level we could simply be in a relationship for years that never brings true meaning or happiness. How many people grow old in loveless or unhappy marriages simply because "they were supposed to?" How has the divorce rate become so high?

I've seen it in both sets of my grandparents. Sure, they might care about each other, but you can always tell the passion died many moons ago. They're constantly annoyed with each other because they never spent enough time to truly accept the faults of the other. As a product of their time, society likely told them the only way to happiness was marriage, and instead of finding someone who was truly compatible they ended up settling for what wasn't visibly harmful. Due to their Catholic upbringing, it's unlikely they'll ever separate. Because of this, they seem to be in a constant cycle of frustration and loneliness. I have always respected my grandparents, but they're a cautionary tale for what happens when we try forcing a partner piece into our jigsaw puzzles.

Look, love is hard. No matter the relationship, compromise is necessary. It's how we function as people. Love "does not seek its own interests." Love "endures all things." In order to love someone, we need to be willing to sacrifice things for the wellbeing of others. That being said, how much compromise is too much compromise? We need to love ourselves 100% in order to love others 100%. If a relationship constantly makes us unhappy, if it never feels fulfilling or never brings us joy, if it's emotionally or physically abusive, that is an unhealthy and condemned relationship. There are certain standards we should all place when picking a partner (which is where the whole "red flags" thing comes up). Obviously, safety is the number one thing to keep in mind. But I'm also talking about other lifelong things.

As a personal example, I only want to marry a Catholic woman. My faith is extremely important to me, and I want to share that faith with my future wife. Things like going to Mass, sharing the same beliefs about the Eucharist and Mary, and certain moral values. You cannot get this from every woman, not even necessarily every woman raised Catholic. Dating a non-Catholic might work in the short-term for me (though I'll talk about the problems with that mentality in a later chapter), but for a long-term marriage where I'm concerned about the life of my kids and my relationship with God, this would not work. I also want to share a hobby I love with my future wife. When we grow old and are retired, I'd love to endlessly yap to my wife about this hobby we love. I think that would make for a lasting marriage. It doesn't have to be specific: it can be Star Wars, comic book characters, backpacking, history. Something that we can continue to have shared experiences until we die. If a woman doesn't meet these two criteria, I can't really see that relationship having a good ending.

All of this is to say I think we need to take relationships much more seriously. Yes, flings can happen and are usually meant as trial periods. It's okay to go on dates with multiple people to see who's the most compatible with you. But we should all be cautious of *why* we're seeking a partner and if a person is truly right for us. Again, too many of us latch onto the first sign of acceptance for fear of being alone. We need to be comfortable being with ourselves. If we aren't happy single, we won't be happy taken. If we can't love ourselves or even understand what love is, how can we expect to love someone else?

Now, Daniel Sloss actually counts how many people break up after hearing his comedy bit. As funny as that is, I don't aim to do that, and the point of this book isn't to separate people. What I ask all of us to do is to think critically about why we're in a romantic relationship or why we're searching for one. If the result has more cons than pros, then something might have to change.

Of course, the Catholic Church would likely refute this point by arguing divorce is wrong and getting remarried is adultery. From a theological standpoint this is certainly understandable. Genesis 2:24 states "That is why a man leaves his father and mother and clings to his wife, and the two of them become one body." Marriage is supposed to be an eternal covenant to each other.

A bride and a groom are supposed to make a promise to stay faithful to each other till death do them part. And obviously this doctrine is set because it knows people will want to be lazy or flee at the first sign of any conflict, no matter how tiny. However, when we enter a relationship with the mentality of The Jigsaw Puzzle, entering this marital covenant is inherently impossible (or at the very least extremely difficult). Because we do this with the mindset that our spouse is for *my* happiness, they complete *me*, it's for *my* benefit. Rather than marrying someone because we truly love them and will do anything for them, we do it to appease societal standards or as a distraction for something we need to fix about ourselves. As Daniel Sloss puts it, we have become so infatuated with the idea of romance that we never actually learn to love ourselves or our spouses. Our partners become pawns to fix some pain or fault in our lives. They become our therapists or first aid kits when they should be our best friends.

In my opinion, this alone would be grounds for annulment. For those who don't know, an annulment is essentially an official pass by the Church for a couple to separate. It basically claims that the marriage was never valid because the couple never had the right intentions going into it. Now there's a lot of bureaucracy behind this, which is why the doctrine has received quite a bit of controversy. And to be honest, I think the Church often teaches this doctrine poorly and often ignores things like domestic abuse, where "don't get divorced because God said so" is a pretty terrible answer to someone who's literally going through hell. But aside from that, I'd argue many marriages would fit the criteria for annulment because one or both parties are entering this marriage simply to "fix themselves" or to satisfy others.

I know a lot of this sounds contradictory so let me finish off the chapter with a quick summary. Because of our world, we are all broken people. Society tells us that in order to make us whole we need a romantic partner. But this is not true. We cannot love others without understanding what love is. What is love? God is love. Or as 1 Corinthians put it, it's a selfless act or relationship that puts the needs of others before our own. In order to understand this, we need to love ourselves. This does not mean indulging in worldly desires or using our flaws as excuses for bad behavior. It's knowing who you are and being part of something greater than yourself. Seeking a partner to appease someone or for surface level pleasure is a recipe for disaster because it is an inherently selfish reason to be in a relationship. You're using that person as a pawn, a means to an end. To love someone is to love them completely. If we go into romance with the viewpoint of "filling our cup" or "completing our puzzle," we will be dooming ourselves to a life of unhappiness. No matter where we are in our romantic journey, we need to analyze who we are, what we seek in a relationship, and if we want a relationship due to a desire to love someone or as a means to an ultimately selfish end.

The rest of this book will showcase how the Jigsaw Flaw has manifested itself throughout time. There are many different methods in which this happens, some of which will be vastly contrasting depending on the political era. But every age tries answering the Jigsaw question in a rather extreme way, one that ends up benefiting the powerful and gives an ultimately unfulfilling answer. Keep this analogy in mind whenever I bring up any romantic or sexual practice. Let's begin by discussing how romance was viewed in the time of Victorian England.

Chapter 2: From the Victorians to Now

I want to use this chapter to debunk a popular misconception. I've seen quite a few people nowadays say things like "love is dying," or "dating used to be better." While there is certainly an argument to be made that dating used to be easier or more convenient, this does not mean it was inherently better by any means. I could venture through the entire history of romance, but to be frank that would take up way too much time, and it wouldn't be helpful because for the majority of history women were simply seen as pawns in the romantic arena. With men having all the power, it was much harder for a couple to truly love each other due to power imbalance. I titled this chapter "From the Victorians to Now" because I've seen people who suggest Victorian courting is extremely romantic. However, this is not true. I believe shows like Bridgerton idealize the concept of courting because it seems like a noninvasive form of dating, one filled with serenading, heart-filled letters, and bold gestures. While I definitely understand why people would like to return to this ideal, this does not show the full story.

Now I need to be clear here, I do not claim that throughout history there were zero instances of couples truly loving each other. In every age with all its problems, people have always found ways to love each other and live perfectly healthy lives. What I am saying is that the answer to the modern romance epidemic is not "returning to the past." The idea of the past might seem enticing, but the reality is that many of those systems of romance were extremely problematic. This chapter will go on a deep dive throughout the past 150 years of romance. While not super vital to every other chapter, this provides important context for why we hold onto certain practices and how those carry-ons continue to be harmful.

Okay, I know I said I wasn't gonna talk about the entire history, but we do need *some* groundwork. Once we left the Garden of Eden, humanity had to survive on its own. We had to fend ourselves from dangerous animals, we had to feed ourselves, and we needed clothing and shelter to protect us. This survival instinct is what drives so many of us throughout time. Our push to protect ourselves and only ourselves makes us selfish. This put men and women in two different groups: men to protect and lead society, and women to raise the children and keep the home orderly. Some would argue going back to these roots is exactly how we're supposed to act, suggesting the closer we get to our animal roots the more natural things are. But humanity is supposed to be above animals, not act like them. Anyways, this "survival instinct" has continued in some form throughout every era. Obviously for most of human history men have tried to use their strength to overpower women and to make them subservient. As we get closer to the 21st Century, the line becomes blurrier as to how much this is pushed in society. This is where the Victorian Era comes in.

The Victorian Era spanned from 1837 to 1901, marking the reign of British Queen Victoria. One of the qualities most recognized about the era were its strict moral and societal standards. Now there are a lot of reasons behind this, but a lot of that isn't super relevant so I'll give the basic "Spark Notes." Events like The Industrial Revolution, constant fighting such as the War of 1812, and a spiking middle class were all directly before this period. With constant change and chaos, it's very likely the people of England just wanted to chill out and return to some sense of normalcy. Of course, the pendulum swung way too far. Thus, the standards for love and social class became very strict. The reason I started with this era in particular is because echoes of those practices continue today, at least in my home country of America. So, what exactly were these practices? First, it's important to understand what a woman's place in society was.

Iwona Sakowicz wrote a detailed article talking about Victorian Courtship based on a popular magazine at the time titled *The Englishwoman's Domestic Magazine*. In the magazine, it details courtship standards of the era, especially through dialogue between young women who submitted their questions and the editors of the newspaper. Much like I stated earlier, there were clear lines between gender roles, with the woman's focus being emphasized in the house while the man's focus was his career. However, the reason for this might be surprising. Iwona says,

> The division of roles into typically feminine and masculine stemmed from the belief that women were physically and intellectually weak. Yet, an interesting fact was the common belief in Victorian England that women were morally superior to men, and this was connected to the conviction of their physical and intellectual inferiority. … The world was seen as dirty, brutal, and often immoral. The home was the opposite, being presented as peaceful and pure. (216)

As we can see, women were surprisingly held in high regard. If women were thought to be pure, it would make sense why society would want to protect this. That being said, this came with the massive caveat of having to adhere to restrictive social standards.

> A lady was to be natural without affectation or pretensions. She was expected to be civil and respectful to everybody without haughtiness or pride. Bravery was listed as an appropriate feature but with a warning against being 'bold or masculine.' A lady had to be feminine in every aspect. (Sakowicz 219)

And of course, a woman practically had no say on who to court. Sure, perhaps there were subtle ways she could gain the attention of a man, but initiating the courting process was entirely up to men. Apparently, many young women asked the magazine how to gain the affection of a young man. Like the Magic Conch from SpongeBob, the newspaper replied, "Nothing." Can we see why this is a huge problem? In those days, a lady had essentially zero autonomy when it came to finding a suitor. One basically had to come to you. And if no one ever did, tough luck. We still often see this attitude today. Men have been taught they are the ones who are supposed to initiate the flirting or dating process. It's not right for a woman to seek guys out, otherwise she's a slut. In my opinion, if you are interested in someone – no matter your gender – you should take the initiative to ask them out. Don't wait for a guy to approach you, he might not be interested in you until you talk to him. This notion of "the guy needs to ask the girl out" has caused massive issues for both men and women. Because if a woman never gets asked out, she'll feel like she's not beautiful. And if a guy never has luck asking women out, he'll feel insecure about himself.

Now yes, Victorian women did end up having a say on whether she'd marry her courter or not. And I don't want to paint this era as completely loveless. In fact, it was seen as quite important. However, this was more of an important factor *after* getting married. Courting was not supposed to be a long endeavor, and the notion of things like "love at first sight" was actually frowned upon. Flirting was deemed suspect, at least in many situations. "The aim of courting was to find a partner for marriage. 'Courtship is the running footman of matrimony' claims one of the manuals poetically." [1] In one perspective, I can agree with that sentiment and even applaud it to a degree. However, the problem is that the marriage is built more around "what is proper" rather than if you truly love someone or have chemistry with them. For a woman, realistically the goal was to be with a man who was well off and would raise her status in society. For a man, realistically the goal was to be with a woman who would maintain his image and would give him heirs. She needed to be "home-loving, innocent, meek, and tender. A strong woman was not a

---

1. Sakowicz, 225

good choice." [2] Dowries were probably an important factor as well. Now sure, the people of the time can claim true love was an essential aspect of marriage. Love letters and gifts were surely important back then as they are now. But let's be honest here, for many the thought of being ridiculed or outcasted simply because you weren't married or because you didn't adhere to the strict standards likely outweighed the quest for true love.

There was a very specific process to courting, and if this wasn't abided it would be seen as extremely improper. "…a gentleman was to appear in public places where he could meet her, such as a church, a park, or a 'place of amusement.'" [3] Once the point of initiation was met, the two would start conversing about their lives. After that, it pretty much all came down to the parents. The guy needed to introduce himself to the parents via letter. Any further communication or meetings needed clearance by the parents. Much like today, the gentleman would ask the father for the daughter's hand in marriage. This control the parents had is probably my biggest problem with this era. The couple essentially have no control over their marriage. Sure, there might be *some* choice about who a man picks, but unless you steered away from societal standards you needed to maintain firm procedures to find love. Is this really the type of culture we want to go back to?

Many facets of Victorian courting continue to this day. It is generally agreed upon that men should be the one to approach a woman. Some women claim this isn't or shouldn't be true anymore, but in all my experience I have rarely seen women go out of their way to make moves on men. I'm not going to provide an answer to this because to be honest I don't know why. All I can say is that we still adhere to that standard of Victorian courting. While not nearly as strict, there are certain guidelines that couples of today's age are asked to follow. This generally involves a first date or hookup, a trial period (aka situationship), the 'I Love You Stage' (where

2. Sakowicz, 223
3. Sakowicz, 221

the two finally acknowledge they're in a committed relationship), moving in together, and finally marriage and/or having children. As I previously mentioned, it is a social standard for men to ask the father for the daughter's hand in marriage. Any deviation from this is usually seen as suspect. Even worse, the situationship phase has many strict standards, as going out to the wrong restaurant or the wrong humor or hobbies is instantly considered a red flag. Furthermore, many women want to be with a guy who is extremely successful, while many men want to be with a woman who will adhere to their every want. There is certainly more autonomy when it comes to a person's choice in partner, but we essentially follow a much looser form of Victorian courtship.

Many of the women who submitted letters to *The Englishwoman's Domestic Magazine* seemed to become increasingly frustrated with the extremely narrow lifestyle they needed to adhere to.[4] Again, women didn't really have a choice in their partners. Enter the Flapper Era. A common theme throughout history is that society exists on pendulums. One extreme standard will lead to an overreaction that leads to another extreme standard. This is very much the case for romance.

So, what led to the end of the Victorian Era? Well, in the most basic way it ended with the death of Queen Victoria, like I described earlier. However, the cultural era arguably continued for about another decade. This would definitively end during World War I. Since the men went away to fight in the war, someone had to keep all the jobs and society running. Women stepped up to the plate to do that. As horrible as the war was, it did give women an incredible amount of freedom and rights they previously did not have. With this newfound freedom in money and career choices, they weren't just going to give that up after the war. This, plus the frustrations from the Victorian Era, led to the flapper lifestyle. Women gave up their corsets for bras and lingerie. They had sleeker dresses than the previously poofy ones, had shorter hair, and applied

4. Pages 220 and 224 best illustrate this.

much more makeup. Drinking and smoking in public was cool. This rebellious spirit was no doubt attractive to some of the men who were likely also tired of the strict standards of the Victorian Era. Another big change was the mass production of Henry Ford's automobiles. This gave young people the opportunity to travel long distances without having to consider the needs of their parents.

This social revolution led to much more sexual freedom among young people in the 20s. There was a much higher emphasis on emotions and chemistry rather than romantic class. This is where another portion of modern dating evolved from. Of course, though the social standards had shifted, that didn't mean they were any less strict. Because now if you weren't engaging in these social activities, no matter how controversial, you would've been seen as weird by your peers. Much like today, if you didn't have sex or didn't go out partying at the speakeasies, you "weren't enjoying life" or were "too conservative and restrictive." And while marriage was still the end goal of the time, ultimately the priority became personal, emotional satisfaction rather than to truly love someone.

From here, society went back and forth on whether to lean into traditional gender and dating norms or to scale back on those practices. With the Great Depression and World War II, people wanted to return to a sense of normalcy. This is where the Nuclear Family came in. While not as crazy as the Victorian Era, there were high standards for how people approached marriage and romance. Traditional gender norms returned, religious views were socially and legally enforced, and strong parental authority came back. Then in the 60s and 70s, the Counterculture Movement swept the youth. This was in response to the standards set by the Nuclear Family. If you've seen Footloose, you'll have a good understanding of what this means. Muck like the Flapper Era, sexual freedom and drug use returned to being a form of rebellious expression by the youth. This was where the concept of marriage was really questioned, with many young people believing free love is the way to do things. Of course, the 60s and 70s were also noteworthy for the Vietnam War, the Civil Rights Movement, and the Second Wave Feminist Movement. All of these changes, combined with a weakened economy, yet again resulted in people wanting that return to normalcy. This is where the Regan Era of conservatism came in, which I'd argue continued until about 2008. Here, dating standards appeared to be similar to the loose courting standards of the 50s. Men were the ones who should approach women. Chivalry was an extremely important factor for what men were supposed to do. Open doors for women, pay for dates, bring flowers as a gift, and walk on the outside of the sidewalk. I think many people want to return to this lifestyle because there were very set standards for dating. Do step one, step two, and so on. There weren't "situationships," and people were (generally) quite open with their intentions when dating. However, I still feel this is viewed through a rose-tinted lens. As with the Victorians, it was still improper for a woman to ask guys out. Though unlike the Victorians, this was more of a penalty against the guys for not "being man enough" if they didn't get women.

When Obama took Office, that's when the pendulum swung back to a state similar to the Counterculture Movement. However, the big difference was social media and online dating. Suddenly, people could connect with virtually anyone in the world through the Internet. Sharing these views on free love and rejecting tradition could be accessed and shared by millions of people. With COVID-19 and all the political chaos as of late, it seems like traditional values are on the rise as people want that sense of normalcy and stability. I fear the pendulum may swing back too far again to the point of women being abused, but only time will tell.

Ok, so why do I tell you all this? Why did we just go through a bunch of history? Because we consistently see several massive issues when dealing with any given time period. In conservative eras, there is a higher focus on sustaining your image and working on love post-wedding. This means there is little to no emphasis on emotion or romantic chemistry. For liberal eras, there is a higher focus on emotional connections and sexual pleasure. However, this hedonistic lifestyle ignores compatibility and commitment. And in both eras, love is selfishly driven. Whether it's your image or materialistic pleasure, there is no importance placed on loving someone.

I was trapped between the end of the Reagan/Bush Era and the Obama Era. I was taught to be a gentleman and to use more traditional means of dating. Generally, this would mean asking a girl for her number or openly expressing my feelings to someone whom I thought was cute. Now, my insecurities started in middle school. This is because there was a Valentine's Day dance we were required to go to. There's no conceivable reason as to why this was mandatory, but the day was basically treated as a school day plus the dance at the end. Anyways, the big thing was "who you were taking to the dance." This was likely propelled by the countless coming of age films and societal expectations that you needed to take someone out to the dance. While never explicitly stated, the message that was put into my brain was "if you don't go with someone, you are a failure." Seemed simple enough, right? Ask someone out and they'll give you a chance, right? Wrong.

Now I suppose one might argue my problem was I didn't ask out nearly enough girls, but having developed crushes - plus keeping in mind I wanted these people to potentially be my girlfriend – I only asked out one girl per year. In seventh grade, I openly asked a girl if she wanted to go to the dance with me. To which she responded, "let me think about it." These words are single-handedly responsible for years of self-deprecation and insecurity. For months, I tormented myself asking myself what in the world I did wrong. Why couldn't she give me a direct answer? Was I not romantic enough? Was I too ugly? Did I need to be her friend first? Was she secretly into me but didn't have the courage to continue? I'd ask her again once or twice, but the answer was the same. If you've ever had this response, you'll know it basically means no. If you're ever in a situation where someone asks you out, please give them a definitive yes or no. Because in an effort to be nice or kind, you essentially leave someone wondering what the answer is, and it kills them to know the answer or what they should be doing to be with you. It leaves too much room for interpretation. Is this silly for a 25-year-old? Probably. But for someone who was only 12 having his first experience asking someone out, it left me extremely confused and discouraged.

Okay, so a year went by, and I moved on to a new crush with a new dance. Last one didn't work out so well, so I decided to try a new strategy. This time, I wrote a love letter. Sounds kinda cute, right? Very reminiscent of that Victorian courtship. Yeah, well that didn't work out either. Now looking back, I can hardly blame the girl for never giving me a response. The way I handed her the note seemed like it would've been a prank. Plus, with how extravagant the words were it probably seemed too silly to be true. But at the time, I thought it was the same situation all over again. Ask out crush, get an unclear response. Again, with how much dances and "needing relationships" were pushed onto me I felt an inherent sense of failure because I didn't do what was asked of me. I wasn't normal.

Freshmen year of high school came, and I tried to have a better/different outlook. However, trying to follow the traditional path of "get girl's number, go on date" never seemed to pan out. There's no real explanation I can give. One theory is that I wasn't forthcoming enough.

Maybe I wasn't clear with my message, or I never used romantic language. Another theory is that my virtue of being chivalrous was simply not what those girls wanted. Now I have always tried to maintain this, as I think being chivalrous is important. Regardless of gender or romance, I think chivalry is an important way to respect others. However, in some regards this might've hurt more than helped. Over the years, I've noticed "the bad boy" is an archetype many young women fantasize about. Some common and somewhat disturbing examples are Anakin Skywalker, Edward from Twilight, and Hardin from the After series. These characters often use very creepy and borderline criminal behavior to get the girl. Yet because of their confidence, charm and rebellious or mysterious aura, they are often seen as attractive. There's also the concept of "fixing men" from their trauma, something I'm sure many women have fallen trap to. Needless to say, I never fit this description due to my lack of serious trauma and my inclination to follow rules.

During my sophomore year, I probably had the worst dating experience in my life. Homecoming dance was around the corner, and yet again people asked me who I was taking (do you see a pattern here?) While we weren't mandated to go to Homecoming like in middle school, it was still deemed as a social necessity to go. As a guy, you just had to ask a girl out and go. And if you didn't you were weird. My friends at the time continued pressuring me to ask out anyone. Now for some context, I went to an all-boys Catholic school. We had a sister school of all-girls, and they were generally the ones guys would ask out. While I loved my high school, one thing I found weird at the time was that in order for the girls to attend our Homecoming, they needed a date to attend. Guys, on the other hand, could go freely. I'm not sure if that's still the policy today, but I think that's a big issue because a) people do just like to go on their own or with their friends. And b) that can lead to a lot of self-doubt for the girls who were never able to find a date.

Long story short, I ended up taking a girl to Homecoming who was a friend of a friend, mostly because of the date rule. I thought it would be kind of me to allow this girl the opportunity to experience Homecoming. And who knows, maybe something could've happened between us.

However, the ensuing experience was a complete disaster. I followed all the steps I was supposed to take. I bought her ticket, took her out to dinner, I got her a corsage, I tried dancing with her, did all the photoshoots and other gentlemanly stuff. But instead of having a shared experience, she instead decided it would be better to run off with her friends. Now luckily the same exact thing happened to another friend of mine, so I wasn't exactly alone, but it was pretty rude of her to just leave me hanging even though I put in all this effort. My Homecoming kinda just turned into eating the appetizers and trying to speak to my friend over the obnoxiously loud music. Pretty lousy if you ask me. If she were upfront with me that she only wanted to go to Homecoming to hang out with her friends, I probably would've been ok with that. But instead, we played this whole song and dance of going out on a date, only for me to eat dirt. My feelings of insecurity started up again. What did I do wrong? I did everything I was supposed to do. I tried making a connection with her. Did I need to be more romantic or forthcoming? Was I too ugly? Was I not interesting enough?

Ok, if it was just a lame date, I probably would've forgotten about the whole experience. However, what really made me mad happened afterwards. Now I only know this because a friend told me, so keep in mind this is from a secondhand account. But I trust what he said is true. So apparently the girl ended up spreading gossip about me and even made a meme making fun of me. I never wished to see the actual contents of the meme, but apparently it had something to do with "how weird I was." Supposedly, I was sus for expressing my love for Star Wars and Sonic. Again, what did I do wrong? Was there some action I did that made her uncomfortable? Did I do something to intimidate her? If I did something seriously wrong I would've loved for her to tell me so I wouldn't make that mistake again. But I never got the answers to my questions. By the time my friend told me this, I lost contact with her. And to be honest, I was too angry to care. Unfortunately, this and other similar experiences from friends gave me a burning resentment for women. All of my prior experiences, all my loneliness and insecurity finally bubbled over and I hated the concepts of relationships in general. It was an extremely toxic anger that almost led me down a dark path of hating women.

Luckily, I was saved by Christ. I know, that sounds really cringe to say. But if it hadn't been for the Gospels and the gift of having an amazing mom, I very well could've become a terrible person. In a way, knowing that Jesus was a single man gave me a lot of courage. On the cross, Jesus felt like the loneliest person in history. He was tortured, hungry, thirsty, physically and mentally distressed, and the world hated Him. He accepted all our sin and suffering and put it onto Himself, with no one to console Him. Getting to understand Christ and His loneliness, only for that to be redeemed in the Resurrection gave me a lot of optimism. By following Christ and letting Him be my Partner Piece, I no longer felt like I needed something external to feel happiness or loved. Christ died for me to be a better person. If I continued down that path of resenting women and relationships, I would be spitting in the face of everything He did. Since my high school days, I've been much better and I view women in a much healthier way. I still struggle and feel lonely every once in a while. But God has given me the strength necessary to navigate life without worrying about my insecurities or feeling the need to have a girlfriend. Even if I'm all alone and have no one to help me, Christ is there to console me and give me the strength needed to move forward. If I follow Jesus, everything will turn out okay in eternal life.

I tell you my background to show why the traditional system doesn't work. Pinning all the responsibility on the guy to initiate the dating process is problematic because guys like me who never seemed to find success blame ourselves for not being in relationships. Clearly there is something wrong with us if following attempt after attempt, different as they may be, we still find ourselves alone and getting rejected. Unfortunately, this brews a lot of insecurity and leaves us dangerously vulnerable to "alpha male gurus" or "love doctors" who manipulate men into joining their programs. Lonely men fall victim to these predatory scams because they're trying to fill a void society forced onto them. Rather than finding strength in being alone, these men are often told women are the problem or that they need to use criminal behavior to "get laid." And that is extremely worrisome.

I know I'm making sweeping generalizations here, but no matter the era people inevitably place themselves into boxes based on the societal standards placed upon them. Thus, we return to the Jigsaw Flaw. The only way we can be satisfied in the confines of our soul is by filling that hole inside us. The Partner Piece. Our Soulmate. But in reality, we need to break away from these boxes we and society place on ourselves. Finding the peace within us, the Joy of the Gospel, enlightenment. These are the things that will truly fill that void in us. Every time period may have its merits in how it views love, but they are an ultimately inadequate solution because they are trying to give an imperfect, human answer. Love was dead in every era. But Christ gives us the opportunity to love not like humans do but as He did. A perfect, selfless, life-giving love. And if we can all follow that format, even if you may not believe in Him, then the world would be a much better place.

Now, there was another reason I went into detail on those moments in history. That has to do with the next chapter: The Commodification of Love.

Chapter 3: Relationshopping

The rise of capitalism is generally thought to have started in the 16th century. This economic system places heavy emphasis on profit through trading and commercialization. AKA, a party gains wealth or capital based on economic trades or business deals. Why in the world do I bring this up? Well, because when living in a capitalistic society, people tend to view everything in life as a commodity. It just makes sense: I purchase a house to live in, I buy food to eat, I pay to watch a movie, I use a loan to get education. Almost everything in life is some form of commodity, that's just how capitalism works. Now I'm not saying I hate capitalism. It is a far from perfect system, but as of right now I think it's the fairest economic structure we have. Because despite all the barriers to entry (some much greater than others), the individual still holds the power to move up and become successful. That should be applauded.

However, this system fails with some very important aspects in life. Not everything should be a commodity. You can't place a price on everything. For example, how much is the movie *Avengers: Endgame* worth? Well, there's several ways to look at this. Is it the budget it cost to produce and market the film? That would be about $400 million. Is it the box office performance? That's about $2.8 billion. How about the cost of a movie ticket? In 2025 that's about $20. What about what the individual thinks it's worth. Someone who loves the movie would probably think it's worth millions of dollars. I on the other hand didn't like two thirds of it, so I'd probably say the movie is worth maybe 100 bucks. You cannot place a monetary value on art because it is an entirely subjective experience. The value of art has to do with an emotional connection to it, something completely abstract. The same goes for nature. Sure, you could try determining its worth based on natural resources to consume, tourism, or property values. But something like Yellowstone National Park or The Great Barrier Reef can't have real monetary value. The same is true for relationships.

Unfortunately, searching for a partner has basically turned into a shopping experience. This has taken on different forms throughout history, which we'll review in a second. But because of our selfish drive to find the perfect Partner Piece, we end up turning people into simple grocery items instead of complex personalities. This is called 'Relationshopping.' The term was first coined in a 2010 study by the same name, written by Rebecca D. Heino, Nicole B. Ellison, and Jennifer L. Gibbs. Now, their paper specifically deals with online dating, but this concept applies to almost every common form of romantic pursuit. One of their main theses argues that when we view the dating landscape like a commercial marketplace, prospective partners are "commodified as products to be sold, assessed, purchased, or discarded." [1] Okay, what exactly does this mean? I'm sure if you're reading this you might be telling yourself you don't view dating like this. This mentality is unfortunately ingrained in our society and it's very hard to escape. I myself fall into this trap a lot. But it's important to understand this concept to see why it is harmful.

In the most basic analogy, potential partners are treated as objects. They become a tool to fix some problem with us. They become a filter to make our image look better. Look at the analogy we've been using: they're reduced to a puzzle piece meant to make us feel good. This is a huge problem. When we reduce a person to an object, it becomes much easier to view them as something to be used, something to be manipulated or controlled. The end goal is to do whatever it takes to satisfy our desires, no matter how harmful. This is the path to the Dark Side.

Objectification has taken on many forms throughout history. Women's value is most commonly based on sexual appeal, while men's value is based on their social standing via money

---

1. Heino, Rebecca D., et al., 443

or power. Net worth is a prime example of this. However, there are more ways people have been commodified throughout the centuries. For a big portion of human history, dowries were very important. A huge factor in determining the suitability of a woman was how big her inheritance was. For women, the suitability of a man was based on his position of influence. In both cases, politics were very important to the marriage ideal as marriages would happen simply to unite houses or clans. This was a means of preventing war, forming alliances, and for trading. As we go into the Victorian Era, this would evolve. Dowries would be put on the backburner, and the suitability of a partner would be based on social standing. The higher your class, the more you would be seen as a good choice. This would often be confirmed with expensive clothes and lavish gifts. With the turn of the century, this would evolve into the modern dating scene. Now, it was all about determining how good the first date was. Again, this was based on purchasing power and the net cost of a date. Whether that be going out to an expensive restaurant, wearing classy fashion, or buying arrays of flowers and chocolate. In the modern era, this looks more like coffee shops or mini golf, but there is still an attached purchase required. You can't just take a walk in the park or sit down at a random bench to get to know that person. There always has to be a purchasable activity or expensive fashion.

The king of purchases is the engagement ring. If you want to get married, you literally have to spend thousands of dollars "to prove your love." Really, the only things needed to get married are the couple and a witness. That's it. But because of corporate greed and the lies of the diamond industry, these rings have become an essential part of getting married. This all started in 1938 when the diamond company De Beers saw a massive dip in diamond sales.[2] They wanted this to change, so in 1939 they began a new wave of marketing campaigns to get the youth to buy diamond rings. And it worked. In 1947, the slogan "a diamond is forever" was introduced,[3] and

2. Francis-Tan, Andrew, and Hugo M. Mialon, 2
3. Picciotto

the result was a boom in diamond sales. The sales of diamonds in the U.S. rose from $23 million to a whopping $2.1 billion between 1939 and 1979. Again, your love is associated with a monetary amount. I feel so strongly about this because you're already wasting thousands of dollars for a fabricated lie and borderline scam. But what makes me even more aggravated is what happens when the relationship breaks up. While there are return policies, this becomes much more complicated if the ring is custom made, if the ring isn't in near perfect condition, or if the girl decides to keep the ring. So, in those cases, the guy has potentially lost thousands just because getting a ring is "what he was supposed to do." It's a similar thing with weddings. A "good wedding" costs thousands of dollars to get a good venue, food and drinks for all the guests, a DJ, all the decorations, and a lavish dress. All this leads to a couple needing to follow societal guidelines to maintain a certain image instead of showing their love for each other. All the rings and glamorous weddings start to feel more like wasted money to appease guests instead of celebrating the union of two people.

Now look, I'm not saying any of these things are inherently bad or that you should avoid them. Sharing a nice meal or going to an event you both like can be a great way to connect with someone. And of course, it's good to be picky in some sense when selecting who you're compatible with. But this becomes a big problem when we associate a person's value solely with net worth. Because instead of loving a person due to their moral values or personality, we select a partner based on qualifications or product descriptions. If they take us to Cheesecake Factory, that's a red flag. If their fashion isn't good, that's a red flag. If they like cats instead of dogs, that's a red flag. If they voted for a certain politician or are affiliated with a certain party, that's a red flag. All of these are things you'd find on an itemized checklist; they don't define who a person is. And how can they? Everyone is a unique and very complex person. I may love Star

Wars, but that doesn't mean I love every movie. I love animation, but that doesn't mean I'm okay with every piece of animated media. I love my country, but I often disagree with its choices and its people. When we view people as an item on Amazon, we don't see the actual person. We don't love the person for who they are; we love an idea of them.

Enter online dating. The way I see it, there are two huge problems with online dating. One, these companies prey off people's loneliness in order to make a profit. One study by Business of Apps suggests that in 2024 online dating apps earned $6.18 billion in revenue. How do they make so much money? Most importantly, through subscriptions. Certain features are blocked behind paywalls so that they push you to buy a subscription plan or other one-time payments to unlock them. Tinder, for example, blocks unlimited swipes, boosted profiles, or access to exclusive matches. Hinge has a paid section called Standouts that highlights potential matches, and in order to connect with them you need to buy a digital currency called Roses. Other features may include ad-free browsing or seeing who's liked your profile.

If any of you have played video games, you'll know how annoying this is. However, it's arguably worse here because now the mindset is that if you want a higher chance of finding love, you need to pay to unlock these features. These companies likely also sell your personal information to earn more revenue. So now you've sold the most intimate parts of yourself to companies looking to seek a profit and, in the process, they cheaply bait you into more payments just for the chance at finding love. If you've been searching for someone your whole life and have had zero luck yet, I can totally see why you would feel desperate enough to pay for these features. And of course, it doesn't make sense for these companies to try and find you a lifelong match. It would mean they would lose customers. So, they use casino style tactics to get you hooked on the app as much as possible. My conspiracy is that they try pushing hookup culture so they can perpetually have customers returning. Or worse, they continue to feed the lie that your lifelong partner "is just a swipe away," so you endlessly swipe hoping to find a partner that will never come. Being single or engaged with hookup culture is profitable for these companies. Sure, they'll advertise a few success stories here and there to maintain their image, but letting you actually find a partner makes them lose a recurring customer. Weaponizing love and people's loneliness in this way is absolutely disgusting and should be called out.

But the even bigger problem is just how much these apps commodify us. We've already talked about how dating has been intrinsically tied to economic value, but putting this into an online format just inflates the original problem. How so? Think about it, how are these apps designed? A profile will have an image, a description of that person, a way to like the profile, and usually it'll come with a tagline of some sort. Sometimes these are funny, sometimes it'll be weird questions that spark a conversation. Often, you'll be able to see multiple images to get a better understanding of that person's personality. If you don't like anything about this profile, you swipe left. Does this sound familiar? The Relationshopping study says that "The functionality and design of online dating sites encouraged participants to adopt a marketplace orientation towards the online dating experience." [4] Online shopping functions in a very similar way. You have the main picture of the item – often with multiple images – a description of that item, the company's slogan, and a way to positively review the item. If anything seems off about this product, you can easily move onto another option.

For both Amazon and Tinder, you essentially have thousands of options you can sift through, each with pros and cons. With all these options, each product needs to stand out in some way. Pretty soon, we're going through these apps basing our interest solely off images or taglines. Essentially, a person's worth is based on how quickly they're able to catch your

4. Heino, Rebecca D., et al. 441

attention, AKA how attractive they are. For men, this is a huge problem as generally there are more men on these sites than women. This means that only the most attractive men get matches while the rest eat dirt. But in either case, we treat "potential partners [as] commensurable, measurable, and comparable with each other." Viewing people as products is dangerous in many ways, but it is also a doomed format for seeking love because people are way more complex than simple profiles. Some might argue "we don't actually view people this way! We know these are just profiles." But when this format is constantly shown to us, it starts to become wired into our brain. Even having never used dating apps, this is something I struggle with. In the past, I have automatically removed any possibility of a relationship with a certain person simply based on superficial things. Dyed hair, their political preferences, if they like partying. While physical attraction is no doubt important, erasing any possibility of a relationship for extremely basic things is quite childish. Because every person is going to have some sort of problem. No one is perfect, we can't have the perfect partner. By trying to find this "ideal woman," I am again trying to fall in love with the idea of a person, not the person themselves. We place value in a person based on physical traits or certain personality features, not their moral standing. There are inherent qualities about a person we should keep an eye out for, like the example I mentioned earlier about wanting to marry a Catholic woman. However, when we view these desires as part of a cheap itemized checklist, we begin to view people as products.

It doesn't stop there though. By commodifying others in these apps, we also commodify ourselves. This is through a "tangible and explicit assessment of one's own perceived desirability in ways less likely to occur with traditional face-to-face communication." [5] In other words, because these apps are built like Amazon where a product has to stand out to be worth checking out, we place those standards onto ourselves. If we don't get any matches, clearly we aren't

5. Heino, Rebecca D., et al., 436

attractive enough. Clearly there's something wrong with our interests. Clearly there's something inherently wrong with us. Can we see why this is a huge problem?

Look, I don't want to insult people who've used dating apps to find love. I know couples in my personal life who met online and had beautiful relationships. It's not impossible or always unethical to find love from these sites. But I caution how quickly society has adopted online dating into everyday life. I fear it only isolates us more and continues to create insecurity for those who use these apps. And all simply for the profit of a few businessmen.

This leads to the most extreme forms of relationshopping. There have been a few trends recently that have become increasingly concerning. When people become desperate for love or human connection, they'll seek any route possible to try finding it. The first is idolizing celebrities. Many men fall for popular streamers online and they give up hundreds or thousands of dollars just for the streamer to simply acknowledge their existence. One man allegedly paid $10k just to hug an OnlyFans creator. Another man tattooed the face of streamer Pokimane onto his arm, with the caption of his tweet saying, "Now my queen can always be with me." Some more depraved examples include the success of Belle Delphine and Sydney Sweeney's bathwater campaigns, Stephanie Matto earning thousands of dollars by selling her farts, and several OnlyFans creators trying to sleep with hundreds or more than a thousand men in one day. Much like the owners of online dating sites, I point the finger at these women for preying on lonely men and using their insecurity for cheap profit. It's not feminism; it's blatant greed.

Likely the most depressing forms of commodification are pornography and the rise of AI girlfriends. In both cases, you are literally searching up or manufacturing someone who will meet your every desire. They are the hottest person with the best personality because you made it that way. There are no barriers to entry since that actress or AI seems to instantly be in love with you.

They are the ideal woman. But this is ultimately a fruitless endeavor because this is not real human connection. It's a fantasy, an illusion that you fabricated. It will never satisfy you because it's only an imitation of love. You are trying to fill that void in yourself that only true love can do. So, by continuing to use porn or AI girlfriends, you continue to devalue yourself and others. If society continues to push these types of programs or behaviors, we will become more and more isolated. We won't know how to interact with others, perhaps to the point that we only view people as tools or shopping items.

I know the most common response to these actions is to laugh at or call people simps. However, I believe this doesn't do anything positive, as the people engaging with this behavior feel there's no other way to find human connection. We should instead pray for them and create communities where people can form thriving relationships.

No matter who you are, what your circumstances are, or what you've done in the past, you have worth. Every single person who has ever lived has dignity. Each person has the image of God in them, so to view them as a tool or a product is not only disrespectful to that person, but it upsets the divine. As I mentioned earlier, seeing someone as less than human inevitably leads to unspeakable horrors being committed in the name of preserving yourself. The selfish drive to advance the self leads a person to do whatever necessary to fulfill that goal. Most of us start out with good intentions. But we continue to let society and fear drive us. Finding a Partner Piece solely to validate the self simultaneously hurts ourselves and others.

Now, there's another way to commodify people that I wanted to devote a whole chapter to. That's hookup culture.

Chapter 4: The Problem with Hookup Culture

While I will devote a part of this chapter to the more obvious use of the phrase, specifically with stuff like one-night stands and online dating, I'd like to give a broader approach to what 'hookup culture' means. Because while meaningless flings are certainly an issue, I believe they are indicative of a wider problem regarding how we view love. I want to preface this particular chapter by saying if you have engaged with hookup culture or any of the other problems I bring up, I do not judge you. No one is above anyone else, and I certainly have many faults of my own. Like I've stated before, society forces us to want romantic relationships or situations. I can hardly blame the individual. However, if we are to solve the romantic issues of our time, we need to get to the heart of the issue.

Okay, it's time to get a bit theological here. I know this will probably turn some people off, but it's important to understand my overall point about the problems with how we view love. And again, this will be talking specifically about straight relationships but I'm hoping this helps those in the queer community as well.

So, what exactly does the Church say about sex, and why has it become such a talking point in our culture? Well, it famously comes from Genesis 2. Specifically, verses 23-24.

"The man said:

This one, at last, is bone of my bones
     And flesh of my flesh;
This one shall be called 'woman,'
     For out of man this one has been taken.

That is why a man leaves his father and mother and clings to his wife, and the two of them become one body."

These lines alone have sprung countless debates over the centuries. However, the Church has always stood firm in its views on sex because it is directly connected to the dignity of a person. Catechism 2334 states "In creating men 'male and female,' God gives man and woman an equal personal dignity. Man is a person, man and woman equally so, since both were created in the image and likeness of the personal God." So, because every person has dignity, since we are all created in God's image, violating that dignity is extremely serious not only because you're abusing a person's life, but also because it's almost like violating the dignity of God Himself. This is why the Church takes sexual sin so seriously. Contrary to how many people teach this doctrine, sex is supposed to be a holy act. In many ways, it might be one of the holiest acts you can do, *if* you do it in the right context. How can that be true when so many Christian representatives have spoken so adamantly against sex? Well, the Catechism provides some nice paragraphs that explain this. Catechism 2361 says,

"Sexuality, by means of which man and woman give themselves to one another through the acts which are proper and exclusive to spouses, is not something simply biological, but concerns the innermost being of the human person as such. It is realized in a truly human way only if it is an integral part of the love by which a man and woman commit themselves totally to one another until death."

Another portion I like is from Catechism 2364, which says,

"The married couple forms the intimate partnership of life and love established by the Creator and governed by his laws; it is rooted in the conjugal covenant, that is, in their irrevocable personal consent. Both give themselves definitively and totally to one another. They are no longer two; from now on they form one flesh."

Essentially, these paragraphs say that sex is important because you are exposing the most vulnerable and intimate parts of yourself. It is such a deep expression of love that you completely give up yourself to provide unending peace, happiness, and security to another person. One might argue it's one of the highest forms of love, a perfect symbol for God's covenant with us and the sacrificial love He gives. God *is* love. So, when you take that and use it solely for personal gratification, it's a complete slap in the face to everything God stands for. You strip a person's dignity away because you are using their vulnerability as a simple tool for selfish desires. It's essentially a violation of love itself (and therefore, God) because you have turned the very representation of love into a game for surface level enjoyment. If you give away your body so willy nilly, what are you saying about yourself and others? You basically claim that a person's very being is a subhuman object used for personal gratification. And this is a grave issue.

Now for all the reasons I've stated, I do not condone sex before marriage. However, it's unrealistic to assume everyone will abide by this. It's certainly not easy to do; I myself have struggled with chastity. But I bring the Church's view on sex to demonstrate why it's important to take it and relationships seriously, because we're dealing with the dignity of people. All of this leads to the massive problem with hookup culture. Before I delve into the traditional use for the phrase, let me expand the definition of a hookup. In this chapter, I'd define a 'Hookup' as a romantic situation where the sole or main goal is the personal advancement or gratification of a person. This is pretty vague, and that's on purpose. As you might already tell, this definition goes right back to what Daniel Sloss explained with the Jigsaw Flaw. With this definition, if you are seeking a partner solely for your benefit, you are engaging in hookup culture. Unfortunately, I think most of our culture functions with this mindset. This can include a wide array of things, many of which we've already discussed. If you're going on dates to make yourself look good, that's hookup culture. If you have one night stands just for the fun of it, that's hookup culture. If you get matches on Tinder to validate yourself, that's hookup culture. Things get a bit murkier with long term relationships since at that point people generally do love each other. However, there can still be problems that arise from this. Swing parties, polygamy, and cheating are all examples of hookup culture because the goal is personal enjoyment. You're not truly devoted to someone if you're throwing yourself away to multiple people. And lastly, engaging with the Jigsaw Flaw could be considered hookup culture depending on the context.

The biggest argument in defense of hookup culture is "you need experience." In this way, relationships are treated like careers. In many respects, this makes sense. First dates are much like interviews to see if you are a match or compatible. Different jobs and relationships have different niches that cater to how they operate. Much like marriage, one hopes to be in the same industry until they retire. And the longer you're in that industry or relationship, the more skills you gain to maintain that. Relationships and jobs can be hard; those skills could be very helpful for navigating them. The easiest conclusion to draw for both things is that you need experience. After all, the higher your position in a company is or the more technical it is, the more skills and expertise are required to fulfill your role properly. And to get those skills or master them, you need to practice. Practice makes perfect, right? However, using this mindset for relationships is problematic. Because now we go back to our original problem of commodifying someone for our goals. A person becomes target practice to better understand love, and if we miss we move on.

I think why some people give this advice is because they've had bad experiences with dating in the past. The reason their relationship works now is because they've learned from their mistakes or the outcome of a past situation, so the conclusion is that they needed to have that prior experience in order to make their current relationship work. This is very understandable, and I don't want to judge anyone based on their life journeys. However, in my opinion this is a coping mechanism to help explain past ills. Do I need to have burned my hand to know touching a hot oven is bad? Do I need to get punched to know fighting causes pain? The odds of you getting it right the first time are probably low, but that doesn't mean we should go through multiple relationships to love properly.

Let me give some examples to clarify. A piece of advice I've been told is you shouldn't marry the first girl you date. This is so you can get a better understanding of who you are so down the line when you do meet your Partner Piece you're prepared to handle marriage. Essentially, this advice assumes there will inevitably be big problems with your first relationship, due to compatibility issues, meeting a crazy person, or having certain preferences your first partner won't have (and not realizing said preferences until you're in a relationship). From a statistics standpoint, this might seem easy to believe because statistically the chances of you getting it right the first time or meeting someone with near perfect compatibility is extremely low. However, let's assume I (or anyone who's never dated) take this advice to heart. I will now be entering a relationship knowing in the back of my head it's going to end. I'm using this person to improve *my* skills and to find out about *me*. I'm preparing for *my* future. Can we see why this is a problem? You're not actually learning to love someone, you're building a resume. You are using someone for personal gain; you get them to learn a trick or two and toss them when it becomes inconvenient. That is not love. You may not even enter that relationship with bad intentions, but if leaving them is the ultimate goal you are not giving your life for them.

Similarly, people often spew the same rhetoric when it comes to sexual encounters. "You need practice to make sure your future spouse will enjoy it." "You need to know what you like." Again though, this is in pursuit of self-preservation. You're coming up with scenarios in your mind worried about your potential partner leaving and how that's going to make *you* feel. Worrying about if you're good enough in bed is selfish because the whole point of sex is to give up all your vulnerabilities and insecurities to give life to your partner. And these worries wouldn't be an issue if you nor your partner haven't had sex before because there's nothing to compare to. Yes, sex is supposed to be enjoyable, but if you truly loved your partner it shouldn't matter "how good they are" because to love someone is to love them completely and to accept them for their flaws. And in this case, flaws that can certainly be worked on.

Another example is cohabitating before marriage. The common belief in society is that after you've dated for a while you should move in together as a sort of trial run for marriage. At first glance, this makes sense as there are things you won't necessarily know about a person until you move in with them. Things like hygienic routines, how messy they are, what temperature they like to sleep at, snoring, and a plethora of other things that could cause conflict. To a certain degree, it's understandable why a person would want to move in with someone to know more about them. After all, isn't that what dating is all about? However, a big problem arises from this. According to many studies, cohabitating before marriage correlates with a higher probability of divorce than those who waited until they were married. One study by Michael J. Rosenfeld and Katharina Roesler found that while cohabitation may help newlyweds adapt to marriage life on a practical basis, the long-term effects will end up harming or ending the marriage. There's quite a bit of research on this topic you can look up online, but the general consensus seems to align with Rosenfeld and Roesler's finds. It's important to note that correlation doesn't equal causation, so this is not to say cohabitation before marriage is an automatic predictor of divorce. However, this points to a greater truth about the problems with cohabitating and other dating habits.

So, why does it seem like cohabitating causes higher divorce rates? As I've previously mentioned, it's supposed to be an extension of dating, right? Well, this all goes back to the problem of viewing relationships as a career. If I move in with a girl "to see if this will work out," I am going in with the wrong mentality. Because the moment things get hard or I don't like a core part of my partner, it's easy to pick up and go. You have that choice to leave whenever you want because there are no financial consequences or kids to worry about. However, carrying this over to a marriage is extremely problematic because you will have the same mindset of wanting to leave when things aren't going your way. This is not love, it's self-preservation. Love is not supposed to be toxic or life draining, but it's also not supposed to be easy. Marriage is hard. Inevitably, life will throw difficulties your way. But to love someone is to love them unconditionally, accepting them for their faults and imperfections.

With all this, I don't want to say you're a terrible person if you've done any of the things I've brought up or that your relationship is doomed to fail. Dating around is fine and can even be good to search for compatibility. But this is why it's so important to know yourself and be comfortable with yourself before going out there. So you treat every potential partner with dignity and respect. Having spent many years of reflection outside the dating world, I know a great deal about what I would like in a partner because it'll be good for both of us. Who knows if my first relationship will be good. Maybe we'll make mistakes, and we'll have to move on. But I'd certainly like to try. It's very important to me that I treat every person, no matter the situation, with the utmost dignity. Because people aren't tools, they are Temples of the Holy Spirit.

Chapter 5: The Incel Rabbit Hole

With the rise of social media, we've seen a disturbing increase in the divide between men and women. This is for a variety of factors I'll touch on in a bit. However, with this comes the dark corner of the Internet many know as 'The Manosphere.' This is a space that preaches a very extreme practice of traditional gender roles where men are dominant and women are submissive. Men are supposed to be extremely fit, rich, and stoic. "An alpha male." Anything less is what's known as a "beta male," someone who is considered cowardly or weak. At best, women are viewed as potential wives whose sole role is to become mothers. At worst, women are seen as evil cheaters who only care about their own interests. Recently, a similar space for woman known as 'The Womanopshere' has emerged, but given I only know about the male experience, that's what I'll be touching on here.

A derogatory term for men who engage with the Manosphere is 'incel.' Men who are called this are generally viewed as selfish pigs who only see women as sexual objects. While I certainly understand this, I think it's important to understand the history of the term. In 1997, a Canadian university student who we only know as Alana created a website called "Alana's Involuntarily Celibate Project." [1] Alana wanted to create a safe space for those who felt sexually or romantically deprived due to social awkwardness, mental illness, or marginalization. It's not that these people don't want to be in relationships, but due to a lot of social factors (both those which I've discussed and some I'll touch on in a bit) they haven't had success at finding love. This is where the term originates. People who find themselves in a similar situation are 'Involuntarily Celibate' or 'Incel' for short. By this definition, I'd probably consider myself an incel. I've always sought love but haven't had any success in finding it. I'm waiting for marriage to have sex, but one could argue I'm involuntarily celibate to romantic relationships. If you've

1. Note: the original page does not exist anymore. Alana has recounted her history in a blog titled *Love, Not Anger*, though as of November 2019 the project has become inactive.

never had luck with romance and the world blames you, it can be extremely hard to leave the bubble of self-pity and loneliness. There's a big shadow of despair because with every failed attempt the chances of finding love seem lower and lower, to the point that even trying seems pointless. I've had this mindset so many times in my life; it's why I have empathy for people who engage with incel culture, because I've held those very same beliefs and fears before. I applaud Alana for trying to create a safe space for like-minded people to vent their frustrations and to find a community to help with their loneliness.

However, after Alana left the website, things took a sinister turn. Slowly, the space became a place to profit off the loneliness and insecurity of young men. Alpha male gurus and love doctors saw a market for "helping these men" and created programs to "fix them." I use quotations because the reality is that these programs spew depraved beliefs about women and "how to get them." This generally involves manipulative behavior that, in some cases, unfortunately leads to rape. For many, the goal becomes to have sex with as many women as possible, no matter how it happens. Because of this, women are reduced to sexual objects that must fit the desires of men. Women are often considered cheaters or gold diggers by virtue of being a woman. To someone on the outside, it might seem extremely obvious that these are predatory scams that promote dangerous ideology. But as someone who has dealt with modern dating life and experienced little success in it, to me it seems extremely obvious why they *would* join these sites.

So, what are some reasons men might be drawn to the Manosphere? Well, I've already described in length how society pushes relationships in an unhealthy way. If you're constantly told you need to be in a relationship to be happy, only to never be in one and be blamed for doing so, then you're going to look for something to change that situation. In a sense, society puts us in prisons, and those desperate enough will believe anything to escape it. Second, I do think modern feminism has played a role in radicalizing young men. For one, many feminists will spew anti-male rhetoric, things like: "we don't need men," "stop toxic masculinity," or "men are the problem." The general answer these feminists provide is that men need to be more emotional or to seek therapy. However, as many young men have tried doing this, they've received backlash by women for doing these very things. "A suitable man is rich, fit, and doesn't cry." "Short guys are bad." "Ick #87 means a guy is problematic." To a lot of young men, myself included, this type of rhetoric becomes really confusing really quickly because we're left trying to figure out what the hell a woman really wants. Men aren't emotional enough, but they shouldn't cry. He needs to have that "rizz," but complimenting a woman is misogynist. Toxic masculinity is the problem, but he has to be conventionally attractive and extremely rich. This is a massive issue. The conclusion many have is that only the top one percent of guys can have success with romance. Like I mentioned in the Relationshopping chapter, this is somewhat confirmed by dating websites where only the most attractive men have success with them. And when a lot of the media being put out there are projects like the Barbie movie or She Hulk – projects that blame men for everything – then it becomes really easy to start having resentment for women. It starts to feel like women only care for superficial things like height or net worth. To be clear, this is not how I view women now, and it is a dangerous philosophy. But as a young high schooler who had zero success with dating, it was much easier to blame women than to try improving myself.

Once a man has reached this conclusion, this is what's known as being 'black pilled' or 'red pilled.' The Manosphere loves using the Matrix as an analogy. Society is the Matrix, and it's out to get men. They are invisible and destined to fail unless they take the red pill and break away from society and its norms. Guys who are lonely will seek answers for why they've had no success with love, and when they come across an influencer who voices their plight, the rabbit hole begins. Now what exactly constitutes a channel or forum as part of the Manosphere isn't so easy to define because simply addressing men's issues doesn't constitute being in the sphere. However, there are a few ways one begins down this rabbit hole. Jordan Peterson is one such example.

Maybe five to ten years ago, Jordan Peterson was what I'd described as a modern-day philosopher. He used a lot of history and interesting analogies to explain why the world works. From time to time, he'd often discuss things like the problem with identity politics and the "crisis of masculinity." These are things I and many other men have observed, and we resonated with his takes. Because of this, he's grown a large audience of young men who liked his classroom videos where he just explains things using science and history. Ironically, he said in one video he actually thought it sucked it was primarily men who watched his videos because a) it confirms his theory about the modern male crisis, and b) because he wants everyone to take away something from his thoughts. While I wouldn't consider his past self to be strictly in the Manosphere, I believe his thoughts on dating and being "anti-woke" could lead some men down that rabbit hole. This is solely based on algorithms telling people to watch similar content, which may or may not get more extreme with their views on masculinity. In recent times, I feel Jordan Peterson has slowly fed into that ideology much more, to the point where his recent book *We Who Wrestle With God* seems to argue that female empathy is a problem. I'd encourage you to read the book to reach your own conclusion, but nevertheless it seems he's unfortunately become more extreme when it comes to "anti-wokeness" and uplifting masculinity.

Another starting point is the countless YouTube channels "fighting woke Hollywood." I used to follow some of these channels because I too was upset by how movies and shows at the time seemed to care more about political activism than engaging storytelling. However, what once started as a good way to call out dumb decisions turned into an echo chamber filled with people constantly hating on everything. While I certainly understand where this anger comes from, these channels have radicalized themselves so much that they argue any movie with a female or minority lead is a problem. Any project with even the most minute political reference is seen as an attack on men that needs to be fought against. This starts to show the militant nature of the Manosphere. Again, it goes back to the red pill analogy. This can lead to a road of self-destruction where you start to hate everything outside a certain framework, in this case the straight, white male. While it's hard to say if these review channels are strictly considered part of the Manosphere, what's clear is that this can become an easy road to more destructive programs or scams.

The height of all this is Andrew Tate. He's a popular influencer who is very famous for promoting traditional gender roles and using the Matrix analogy. Tate has done this through countless videos on social media and promoting programs to "get rich quick." Lonely men resonate with his views because Tate is one of the only people voicing their frustrations. These men believe he has the answers given his wealth and charisma. However, Tate uses this despair to scam his followers into his predatory programs. While they might contain some good information, these programs are generally built so that Tate's followers are perpetual customers that can never leave. They are reprimanded for exiting the program or speaking up against these beliefs. Most of the content is either free elsewhere, useless, or dangerous. One such program was called the PHD or 'Pimpin Hoes Degree.' In this program, men were taught to use manipulative tactics, often associated with sex trafficking methods like the Loverboy method. This is a deceptive tactic where people are groomed into a relationship. It seems to start normally where the controller shows empathy and gives their partner countless gifts and promises of a better life. However, once a woman gets attached to this relationship, she becomes trapped. The 'loverboy' starts controlling their partner through isolation, threats of violence, and other forms of emotional manipulation to make their partner dependent on them. Andrew Tate and his brother allegedly took part in a human trafficking scheme, so it comes as no surprise that Tate teaches this tactic. Unfortunately, he is only one of many influencers who uses these scams to prey off young men.[2]

As a young boy who was desperate for a girlfriend or physical attention, these alpha male gurus were enticing. They have all these pictures surrounded by luxurious cars and hot women; clearly, they were doing something right. If they could tell me "the secrets to getting laid," then maybe I'd stop feeling so lost. If these love doctors showed me the tactics every successful guy used to get women, maybe I'd finally find my Partner Piece. Perhaps I'd stop feeling so useless.

This is a dangerous road to go down. Using these controlling behaviors to target isolated men and teaching them violence against women is disgusting and reprehensible on every moral level. This is why it is so important to love yourself first and to avoid the lie that needing a relationship makes you happy. Because not doing so can lead down a destructive path. There have been instances of men who consider themselves incels openly gunning down innocent people as revenge for getting rejected. One of the most famous examples was that of George Sodini. In August 2009, 48-year-old George Sodini went inside an LA Fitness in Pittsburgh, Pennsylvania. He entered a women's aerobic class and proceeded to gun them down. Three women died, nine others were injured, and the shooting ended with George Sodini taking his life.

---

2. For more information about Andrew Tate's schemes, watch Coffeezilla's videos, which are listed in the Works Cited section.

For decades, he built up so much resentment due to his failures in the dating world. Sodini bought a program that would help with dating (very likely a predatory scam) but had no luck with it. He would chronicle his frustrations online by saying "Who knows why? I am not ugly or too weird. Girls and women don't even give me a second look ANYWHERE. Women just don't like me."

Another such case was that of Elliot Rodger. On May 23, 2014, Elliot Rodger committed a mass terrorist attack in Isla Vista that resulted in the death of six people, injuring 14 others. Much like so many other men, Elliot was socially awkward and had very little success with dating. As his resentment built up, he'd write a manifesto and post YouTube videos describing his frustrations, specifically against women. This all boiled over on May 23rd as he stabbed his roommates and their friend. He then went to a sorority house with plans to burn the building down. However, unable to enter the building, he decided to shoot three women who were nearby. Rodger continued causing chaos in the city by driving around and gunning down or ramming random pedestrians. The incident ended by Rodger shooting himself while driving, injuring a cyclist in the fallout, ending with the car crashing into a parked vehicle.

You have to be led to such a dark place in your life for it to seem like the only answer to solving your problems is murder. Obviously, the actions of these men are inexcusable on every level. But rather than laughing at these men and avoiding them, we instead should be reaching out to help them. The world has bogged them down so much that they are stuck in the darkness. How many more tragedies must happen before we take this problem seriously? We should provide the light of Christ and community to these people. That way, everyone can truly understand what it's like to have peace and love in your life.

Chapter 6: The Jedi Approach to Attachments

While many of my thoughts on romance come from personal experience and reflection, Star Wars has unironically helped me understand my views. And this is probably because Jedi philosophy aligns so well with my Catholic upbringing. I hope this chapter will be fun for you Star Wars fans out there!

There's a lot of discourse and misinterpretation of how the Jedi view emotions and attachments. I blame this on the extremely poor writing of the Prequels that doesn't properly explain what George Lucas was trying to say. This is because the Jedi often come off as emotionless stoics who are too strict with their dogma. However, if we look at Lucas' interviews, we have a better idea of what he was trying to portray. Let's begin with a quote from a meeting during the production of *The Clone Wars*.

"The core of the Force… I mean, you got the dark side and the light side. One is selfish, one is selfless, and you want to keep them in balance. What happens when you go to the Dark Side is it goes out of balance, and then you get really selfish, and you forget about everybody. And then ultimately yourself because when you get selfish you get stuff. Or you want stuff. And when you want stuff and you get stuff, then you're afraid someone is gonna take it away from you. Whether it's a person or a thing or a particular pleasure…. Then you start to become angry, especially if you're losing it. And that anger leads to hate. And hate leads to suffering. Mostly on the part of the person who's selfish because you've spent all your time being afraid of losing everything you've got, instead of living.

Where joy, by giving to other people you can't think about yourself. And therefore, there's no pain. But the pleasure factor of greed and of selfishness is a short lived experience.

Therefore, you're constantly trying to replenish it. But of course, the more you try to replenish it the harder it is, so you have to keep upping the ante. You're actually afraid of the pain of not having that joy. So that's ultimately the core of the whole Dark Side [and] Light Side of The Force."

So how does this translate to the movies? Well, to become a Jedi you need to take an oath to have no attachments. The belief is that by strongly holding onto something, AKA an attachment, you are going down the Dark Side. Why? Because as George Lucas explained, attachment turns into obsession, which leads to a selfish desire to keep that attachment no matter the cost. This attachment could be a wide variety of things, and this attitude has led to numerous atrocities throughout the ages. Money, political power, land/resources, drugs, food, technology, social media, and perhaps most importantly, relationships. I think people have a hard time understanding that last one because our connection to people is a vital part of life. After all, it's the main topic of this book. However, it's unfortunately very easy to view relationships in a selfish way. By wanting to stay happy for as long as possible, we try to keep the joy of being with others. We conflate that joy with the mere presence of another person, when in reality that joy comes from us sacrificing our needs for their happiness. I've already discussed in length how dating and relationships are commodified. This is an extension of our selfish desires to maintain our state of mind. Relationships become more about what a person can do for us, rather than what we can do for them.

This is why I love Star Wars. It understands the consequences of being selfish and that we can get immense joy from serving others. Jedi can still have friends and be involved with a community. But they place their priorities on serving the needs of the people in the galaxy, not fleeting desires they may have. Of course, the Jedi Way is applicable to any type of attachment, but this book is primarily about romantic relationships, so I'll keep it in theme. Luckily, the story of Darth Vader is the perfect story to explain this very concept.

Anakin Skywalker grew up on Tatooine as a slave. It was a pretty rough life, as he had long, grueling hours working for his master. However, he had his mother to console him. When Anakin was nine, Jedi Master Qui Gon Jinn visited Tatooine and ended up freeing him. This was because Qui Gon believed the young Skywalker might've been the prophesized Chosen One who'd bring balance to the Force. Anakin also dreamed of becoming a Jedi Knight who'd free all the slaves. However, for reasons outside Qui Gon's control, he was not able to free Anakin's mother. Reasonably, Anakin worried for his mother and wanted to return to free her. Things took a turn for the worse when Qui Gon died at the hands of Darth Maul. I believe that Anakin's time as a slave, his increasing worry for his mother, and the lack of a parental figure made Anakin extremely vulnerable to the Dark Side. What started off as a selfless mission to love and free slaves would soon turn into a selfish desire to gain power.

When Anakin was 19, he fell in love with Padme Amidala, Senator of the planet Naboo. This happened when he was sent on a mission to protect her from assassins. Putting aside a lot of the cringy dialogue such as "I don't like sand," the two formed a very real connection with each other. However, Anakin began having dreams of his mother dying. Believing his mom's death would come to pass, he quickly (and discreetly) went to Tatooine to see what was happening. He learned that she was kidnapped and killed by the Tusken Raiders. After finding his mother's body in their camp, he slaughtered the entire village. And not just the men, but the women and the children. From here, we begin to see Anakin's turn to the Dark Side. He wanted to become the most powerful Jedi, one that would free the galaxy of every pain imaginable. He gained an obsession over Padme. When he started getting dreams of her dying in childbirth, he made it his mission to prevent this from happening. He wanted more power, even over life itself. What started as a budding romance turned into an addictive grasp over her. Anything outside Padme's undying devotion and life was unacceptable.

Palpatine saw all this and groomed him for years on end. When the time came, he revealed himself as a Sith Lord to Anakin, manipulating Anakin to believe the Dark Side could save Padme. Thinking the Jedi Way couldn't help him, he submitted himself to Palpatine and became Darth Vader. From there, he would help subjugate the galaxy in the hopes of "saving it" and "protecting Padme." However, Padme saw all that Anakin was doing and couldn't support him. He was going down a path she could not follow. When Padme rejected Anakin and his actions, he violently turned on her. He used the Dark Side to Force Choke her, which resulted in her death. From there on, Darth Vader would lead a lonely and miserable life.

I'm sure we won't all become dictators because we were too obsessed with our loved ones. But Darth Vader's story is a cautionary tale about what happens when we approach our romantic relationships through a selfish lens. When dating is motivated by our selfish desires, we cling onto our partners with such a strong grasp that the reasons we entered that relationship fade away. We stop giving and start taking. We stop loving and start worrying. Worrying they'll leave us or that we won't be good enough. Fear is the path to the Dark Side. Fear leads to Anger. Angry at ourselves for not being better, Angry at our partners for not putting us first. Anger leads to Hatred. Hatred for them for not doing what we asked. Hatred toward ourselves for not clinging hard enough. And hatred... leads to suffering. Domestic violence, drug abuse, depression, stalking, rape, and many other sins.

I'm not at all suggesting we all be like the Jedi and forego romantic relationships. But we should always be mindful about *why* we're in one or seeking one. Is it because we truly want to love someone and bring joy into their lives? Or are we trying to fill a void in our hearts, using someone to fix our problems. It can be a blurry line but messing that up can lead to a life of pain and loneliness.

To end this chapter on a positive note. I do want to conclude the story of Darth Vader. In probably the most famous scene in all of Star Wars, Vader's son Luke Skywalker confronts him and the Emperor in *Return of the Jedi*. After a grueling lightsaber duel, Luke has the opportunity to kill Darth Vader once and for all. However, because of Luke's love for his father – and because he knows he'd fall to the Dark Side in killing him – he puts down his lightsaber and spares Vader's life. Luke becomes a Jedi like his father before him. Enraged, the Emperor blasts Force Lightning onto Luke. This seemingly endless torture nearly kills the new Jedi. Luke screams out to his father to save him. In a final act of sacrificial love, Anakin grabs the Emperor, electrocuting himself in the process, and throws him down a shaft. This ended up not only in Luke's life being saved, but the freedom of the entire galaxy. Thus, Anakin redeems himself and brings balance to the Force. Anakin's sacrifice reconciles the father and son, with a mutual understanding and love for each other. The injuries from killing Palpatine result in the death of Anakin Skywalker.

His final act of sacrificial love for Luke is exactly the Christ-like love we should all aim to have. Luke and Anakin loved each other not because there was anything to gain for themselves, but because they sought the salvation of the other. This is the key difference between Anakin's love for Luke and Padme. If we can all learn to love like this, if we're all a little less selfish and try to be a little more giving, then the world would be a much better place.

Conclusion: A New Hope?

Truth be told, I'm not sure how many people this book will reach… if any. And sadly, even if this book somehow causes this massive cultural shift, all the problems I talk about in this book are ones that will be around for the rest of human existence. No matter who or where you are in life, even if you're asexual, society will try to force some norm of romance onto us. Every individual will be forced to ask themselves these same questions about happiness and dating. But there is hope! Each of us has the power to break the chains that hold us down. Everyone has the ability to find peace in their hearts in the midst of trial and tribulation. Whether that's religion, spiritual enlightenment, or self-discipline, we each hold the key to our own happiness. You just have to unlock it.

Let's do a quick recap before closing the book. In this fallen world, we are all broken. With that brokenness, we all seek happiness because the world creates a void in our hearts. However, society tells us that joy can only come when you're in a romantic relationship or having sexual encounters. As Daniel Sloss puts it, we're told that to complete the Jigsaw Puzzle of our lives, we need a Partner Piece as the center of it. This is flawed because this leads us to use people as tools for our happiness. And because no one is perfect, nothing about that relationship can give us true peace because people love imperfectly. But because we're afraid of losing our fleeting pleasures, we cling onto our romantic attachments. That fear leads to anger, which leads to hate, which ends with suffering. The result is an array of societal problems that are the result of commodifying people. This can be anything from hookup culture, online dating, cohabitating, predatory scams, or ultimately using people as target practice. All this leads back to our original problem of trying to seek joy.

First, we must learn to love ourselves. If we cannot do this, then we won't know or have the capacity to love others. Breaking from the constraints of society and being comfortable with yourself ensures that you don't need another person to feel loved. Furthermore, it's by understanding what love is, as Christ loved, that we can truly understand how to love ourselves and others. This is not a selfish or obsessive attachment like how Anakin felt about Padme. Rather, this is a sacrificial love that only seeks to uplift the other. Much like Anakin and Luke loved each other, we should all aim to give of ourselves to ensure the happiness of others. As 1 Corinthians 13: 4-8 says,

> "Love is patient, love is kind. It is not jealous, it is not pompous, it is not inflated, it is not rude, it does not seek its own interests, it is not quick tempered, it does not brood over injury, it does not rejoice over wrongdoing but rejoices with the truth. It bears all things, believes all things, endures all things. Love never fails."

If we can all practice this, in and outside of romantic situations, then we and the world will be filled with much more joy and inner peace.

I want to take this time to thank you for reading! I've had these thoughts in my head for a long time and my journey to finding peace has been long and hard. And truthfully, I'm still on that path. I write this book to hopefully help someone navigate the struggles of dating in a world that pushes it so harshly without thinking of the consequences. If I can help even one person, that'll be enough. Remember, you are loved. You don't need to be in a relationship to be happy. You have the power inside you to find your own happiness.

God bless and May the Force be With You!

Works Cited

Alana. "My History with Involuntary Celibacy." *Love, Not Anger*, 8 Oct. 2019,

https://www.lovenotanger.org/my-history-with-involuntary-celibacy/.

Burns, Michael. "Online Dating: Are We In Hell?" *YouTube*, uploaded by Wisecrack, 18 Feb.

2022, https://www.youtube.com/watch?v=-bcKRd_lfAg&t=919s.

Catholic Church. *Catechism of the Catholic Church.* 2nd ed., United States Catholic Conference,

2000.

Curry, David. "Dating Apps Revenue and Usage Statistics (2025)." *Business of Apps*, 6 June

2025, https://www.businessofapps.com/data/dating-app-market/.

"Exposing Andrew Tate's Crypto Grift." *YouTube*, uploaded by Coffeezilla, 19 Oct. 2024,

https://www.youtube.com/watch?v=e4UJE8XbrUs.

"Flappers." *History*, 6 Mar. 2018, https://www.history.com/articles/flappers.

Francis-Tan, Andrew, and Hugo M. Mialon. "'A Diamond is Forever' and Other Fairy Tales: The

Relationship between Wedding Expenses and Marriage Duration." 15 Sept. 2014.

Gelles-Watnick, Risa. "For Valentines Day, 5 Facts about single Americans." *Pew Research

Center*, 8 Feb. 2023, https://www.pewresearch.org/short-reads/2023/02/08/for-valentines-

day-5-facts-about-single-americans/.

Heino, Rebecca D., et al. "Relationshopping: Investigating the Market Metaphor in Online

Dating." *Journal of Social and Personal Relationships*, vol. 27, no. 4, 2010, pp. 427-447.

"I joined Andrew Tate's cult and it was worse than I thought." *YouTube*, uploaded by Coffeezilla, 1 Aug. 2022, https://www.youtube.com/watch?v=BijOF8I2t_4.

"Jigsaw." Daniel Sloss: Live Shows, season 1, episode 2, 11 Sept. 2018. *Netflix*.

Lucas, George. "George Lucas Explains the Force: The Light Side and the Dark Side." *YouTube*, uploaded by The Andrew K Channel, 14 Oct. 2018, https://www.youtube.com/watch?v=wiImoO5QkcA.

Pascal, Blaise. *Pascal's Pensées*. New York, E.P. Dutton & Co., Inc., 1958.

Picciotto, Eleonor. "De Beer's Most Famous Ad Campaign Marked the Entire Diamond Industry." *The Eye of Jewelry*, https://theeyeofjewelry.com/de-beers/de-beers-jewelry/de-beers-most-famous-ad-campaign-marked-the-entire-diamond-industry/.

Rosenfeld, Michael J., and Katharina Roesler. "Cohabitation Experience and Cohabitation's Association with Marital Dissolution." *Journal of Marriage and Family*, vol. 81, no. 1, 2019, pp. 42-58.

Sakowicz, Iwona. "Victorian Courtship – from Ideal to Real. The Englishwoman's Domestic Magazine and the Rules of Etiquette." *Studia Historica Gedanesia*, vol. 14, 2023, pp. 215-227.

The New American Bible. Revised Edition, Catholic Book Publishing, 2011.